Wisdom of Shadows & Light

LUCY CAVENDISH

Artwork by JASMINE BECKET-GRIFFITH

BLUE ANGEL®
PUBLISHING

Wisdom of Shadows and Light

Published by Blue Angel Publishing
80 Glen Tower Drive, Glen Waverley,
Victoria, Australia 3150
E-mail: info@blueangelonline.com
Website: www.blueangelonline.com

Text by Lucy Cavendish
Artwork by Jasmine Becket-Griffith
Edited by Catherine Smith

Blue Angel is a registered trademark of Blue Angel Gallery Pty. Ltd.

ISBN: 978-1-922161-27-7

From the ashes, a fire shall be woken, a light from the shadows shall spring; renewed shall be blade that was broken, the crownless again shall be king.

J.R.R. Tolkien

Introduction

Bittersweet...Unheard...Unconventional...Rebellious...
Cheeky...Whimsical...Invisible...

They're not words you often hear associated with the spiritual world, are they? Nevertheless, some of the most spiritual beings who have ever lived are those who have been most at odds with what we call the "mainstream". They do not fit in. They have had moments of despair. And they know being truthful, and being real, is one of the greatest strengths and spiritual paths of all!

So, with this book, they ask you to step out from the shadows, to no longer hide your light away, and acknowledge your individuality and strange genius! Likewise, the beings you will discover here are coming out from their own hidden realms, too. They have smuggled their wisdom through to us in stories, history, fairytales and folklore: but they are as real and as powerful as the glorious ones of the celestial realms.

No more shall they hide in the shadows! With the magick of this beautiful book, these shy ones can now reach out and share their message. Welcome to their mysterious world of magick and beauty, where dreams are stranger than reality, but oh-so-likely to come true when you awaken to your own power.

And when we call on them, something fascinating and wonderful begins to happen. For this book is like no other: It is for the lost and lonely, the broken-hearted and the orphans and misfits – for the wanderers and the strangers even in the midst of friends.

Think of this book as an oracle that you can turn to for messages of wisdom and guidance from the beings of Shadows & Light that grace its pages. Before consulting them, set aside some sacred space. This can be as simple as just intending for it to be so. If there is more time, you may like to retreat into a quiet space, light a candle and take a moment to still your mind. When you are ready, hold the book between your hands, close your eyes and think of a question for the oracle or a situation that you'd like to have some insight into. Then open the book randomly at any page, or flick through the pages until it feels right to stop. The being/s on the page you open to will have a powerful message for you to receive in that moment. Take time to connect with the beings in the images themselves as well as reading and reflecting on their message to you.

Wisdom of Shadows & Light is brimming with energies delivered straight from sweet little ghosts who haunt misty pumpkin patches, spooky trick-or-treaters who knock at your door, indignant angels, strange witchy sisters and grumpy fairies busy mending hearts. The messages, images, and realms of this unique book overflow with all that is beautiful, quirky, haunting and shadowy-sweet.

For this book embraces those who have long felt they have no home: this book seeks out the strangelings, the in-betweeners who've seen it all, and now wish to share their wisdom with you. If you are brave enough, asking their advice can reveal a world of sweet beauty, whimsical rhymes and steadfast courage. So say farewell to fear! Walk through the veil, and be prepared to enter their magical world.

The beings of Shadows and Light are here to show you the hidden away aspects of your own soul, to invite you to rediscover childhood dreams and memories, to ask you to speak the truth, and be wholly yourself, without fear of any consequence other than greater freedom and joy!

They will encourage you to acknowledge when you are sad: and too often we ignore the messages coming through from the most powerful and beautiful of sources. Too often, we ask advice from the same sources, again and again.

We know of the Archangels, and of the wisdom of many gods and goddesses, and of intergalactic beings...but what of the soft and shadowy voices that linger in the corners of our own world? What if we were to tune in and be aware of what and who may be around us? What if we took a different route to work this day, or paid attention for the first time to that playground we walk by each day? What if we got out of our car and looked out into the open fields, or stared across the sea, and felt the energies around us?

What if we just tuned in to the world of shadows and light that is all around us?

If you did, I know who you would find. Little ghosts, with messages to share, grumpy angels who have shown you too many times the way forward, and some messengers from hidden realms, showing you are allowing your energy to be stolen, or your courage to fail you. This is the book for when you need to tune in to right-here-and-right-now, to the beauty and strangeness of your own life, with its own unique wisdoms.

This book is a portal to another world, but one which will seem strangely familiar. It is a world characterised by neither the blinding "goodness" of the purely angelic world, nor the dark mysteries of the underworld. It is both, and all the in-between shades and hues, too. Within it dwell beings who have wanted for so long to share their odd wisdoms with you. These are the outcast aspects of your own self, and by tuning in to them, and making a place for them in your own life, you too will begin to remember the strangeness of your own soul.

The Ghost of the Pumpkin Patch speaks:

"Something that is a blessing is being overlooked.
It appears cloaked and seems almost invisible to you.
You must stand in your field – that is to say, your
life – and look around you, and see all that has been
given to you again, and give thanks for it.
You are forgetting how much you truly have, and
how much you will have again, and again.
My time is the harvest: it is now your time to bring
in, or harvest, the joy and love of what you have so
much of, and share your abundance."

The Absinthe Fairy speaks:

"You know how it is… you start having a glass of wine after dinner each evening, then before long, one becomes two, then two becomes three. If you do not drink alcohol, there is another addictive substance tempting you at the moment: food, or negative thinking, or even gossip. While all these addictions can be delicious, they always leave a sour aftertaste, and a guilty energy remains for too long. If I have turned up in your life, know that my gift to you is awareness of an addiction, a temptation you are convinced may be harmless. I am here to point out to you that they are powerful, that you are currently vulnerable, and you can change your life by refusing to fall under their spell. I am your signal to find support for living in clear, bright ways that do not leave you feeling drained, disoriented and disenchanted."

Sea Beacon Fairy speaks:

"I do hold up the light – but only you can choose as to whether the direction I will lead you in is the right one for you at this time. It may be your salvation I lead you to – and it may be that I am gathering souls and you will perish upon rocks, or drown in cold seas. I know this is hard to hear... It is not a sure thing, this advice and guidance you have received, and for all its insistence that it "comes from the light" I want you to know that all of those who do work in the light, are not those who you need to follow at this time. I understand this may be confusing. But I am assuring you mostly of one great truth. That perhaps, you must find your own way out at this time."

The Snow Angel speaks:

"Hmph! There. If they miss that sign, I really don't know what will convince them! Maybe I should just stand here a while, and wait till they notice me, point to the sign, flap my wings, and then they'll believe that it is really a sign! I leave signs for all to see, clear indicators of my presence, and even make my shape in this cold snow, but again and again they ask, Where are my angels? And here I am. I will continue to leave my mark, in the snow, with a feather falling from the sky, in the gentle voice that speaks to you at night, and even in the gentle prod I may give to you from behind! But stop asking for signs!
You have received so very many, and none of them will be seen or acknowledged until you are willing to believe that we are always with you!"

The Trick-or-Treaters speak:

"We may look dark and scary to some, but truly,
we are also fun and peace-loving magical ones!
Don't judge everyone by their appearance: instead,
understand what lies beneath, and discover what
it is they want, and then feel out for any strings
attached. We want you to exercise your feelings: your
clairsentience: the ability to know, and not to rely
upon appearance for your signals.
Then we would like you to meet with us so we can
share our experiences with you, and hear more of
your story too!"

Autumn speaks:

"It is time to stop relying on others for that comfort, warmth and sustenance that only true self-love and acceptance can bring. Waiting for others to offer what you need could be a long and lonely, bone-chilling wait at this time. So you need to look at the resources you have, symbolised by the red apple in my hands. Save your seeds of self-love and plant them. From this magickal apple – your own inner resources – comes the gift of wisdom, of self-love, of abundance and of the knowledge that you are worthy of your own care, love and support. Once you bite into the apple of your inner wisdom, you will be free of the need for approval, shelter and rescue from others. Go ahead! Eat the apple! And discover how amazing you truly are."

Poe speaks:

"Tick-tock, tick-tock, times are a-changing, and I know you too will change with the times, and yet remain entirely yourself! You will be at once of the ancient past, and of the new world which is coming, swift as the train that steamed towards me, making me gasp in wonder. Plan carefully, knowing that when you choose to make use of the new technologies, it will be fearlessly, gracefully, and with integrity. All that changes can be put to wholesome, good and sacred use. The destructive capability of industrialisation and pollution and mechanism is one you understand too well. But you also know that some of the changes to choose from can be used for good – not evil! It is time for you to discerningly embrace the technologies that will allow you to realise your dreams!"

The Grumpy Red Fairy speaks:

"I want to be me, and be free, without everyone
giving me their opinion! I like being different.
I won't be changing, unless I want to! I don't need to
change to fit in – I only "need" to be true to me.
And the people who think I should be smiling,
or wearing a pretty dress, and stop messing with my
hair – they can just deal with it! Some folks do gasp
at tattoos, piercings, black clothes...but guess what?
Some of the world's scariest looking people are the
kindest and sweetest on the inside. You, too, are
fiery, playful, defiant and lots of fun. Be you.
Be rebellious, even. Who's to say how you should
look, or behave? Conformists – that's who! Let's burst
their boring bubble and go wild!"

The Three Witchy Sisters speak:

"We can sense around you some strange energy,
and we three are tuning in so we can identify and
explain to you what it is happening in a wave of three
very clearly, very simply, and without any fear at all.
Because this problem may not even be a problem!
It is simply something you do not understand yet.
Let us come in, let us help you, and we will soon
share exactly what it is. But you must help us by
being aware, awake, and alert to what is around you!"

Eclipse Mermaid speaks;

"This energy shift you are about to experience needs preparation...no effort, no force, but it helps to be ready! Expect amazing dreams, possible clairvoyant experiences, and please do watch addictions, food, alcohol and cigarette (ab)use especially. This is a magnificent time to start a new health regime, particularly if you are wishing to reduce addictions that are unhealthful.

Remember, there's no real avoiding life and the planet's and the galaxy's energy shifts. We can work with these eclipses and maximise their amazing power, or we can do nothing, and their changes could overwhelm us. The worst choice is to fight the energy, and refuse to try something new. What will you choose as your own personal eclipse approaches?"

The Dried Flower Fairy speaks:

"Do you remember that time when you played with the fairies in the garden? Do you remember when your imaginary friend was more real than your own parents? What of the first time you ever noticed your shadow quivering in the light? Swam in the sparkling sea? Kissed your first boyfriend? When you were given a gift for no reason? Hugged by a friend? Had a perfect day? Found messages from angels in the clouds? You seem to have forgotten all the precious moments, so I've been busy gathering them up for you. I now return them to you, so your sadness can be transformed. Let happiness, bliss and gifts for no reason become possibilities you believe in again! When I see you smile, and treasure a moment from the past in the present, I know my work has been done!"

The Winged Seer speaks:

"As so many people hide the truth, even from themselves, it can be hard to receive a visit from me, because I will help you see when someone is camouflaging and half-telling truths, and you will also have insights that seem to come from supernatural sources. It is as if you have changed sight: you can see further, higher and more deeply within. You will experience flashes of future, sudden understandings of the past, and you will be able to foretell likely outcomes. I am the eye of Ra, recreating your future, and the Adrinka, the protective eye, that watches over you while you sleep, and if you follow through on what you now clearly see, there will be illumination, victory and wisdom. Trust that sacred Sight."

Kali speaks:

"I am the dancer who moves through the fire, who wields my sword and severs the cords of energy that entangle you, and who is not afraid of the death that needs to happen. Every act of destruction is an act of creation, and this is no act of pointless destruction and brutality. I am clearing all that is leeching off your energy, draining your strength, and abrading those relationships that cannot do anything but keep you stuck. Whether you realise it or not, you called on me, and I have come to clear the path, to destroy that you have longed to let go of. Something's time has come. And it will be born again, as nothing ever truly dies, it only changes. And that time has come! I am pure fire energy, and the great mother, and as I dance, the death you face brings you to new life."

Marie Masquerade speaks:

"Someone is about to invite you to be involved in something very intriguing. And they will ask you in ways that are ever so charming, so the temptation will be ever so strong. Because they are beautiful, and talented, and powerful you are flattered! But the truth is, you run the risk of paying a very high price for this brush with fame or glory. Be sure that the politics and the intrigues are ones you truly wish for in your life – because there is often a sacrifice that must be made, and many consequences are currently hidden from you. It is tempting, no doubt. But it may not be within your best interests to pursue this strange, slightly tainted offer that will be made."

The Mildew Fairy speaks:

"It always shocks me when people think something "shouldn't be there"...like me! I grow naturally where it's warm and wet, and I love to show you what you may need to take care of. I can do wonderful things: I can be medicine and I can be a parasite too. But all the time I'm showing you what is going on, what you need to change, and whether the conditions are a little too steamy for you! If they are, you can freshen up your environment naturally – don't clean or use harsh chemicals or bleaches as you'll kill all that is helpful and good! You see, I turn up when something is unhealthy and you just aren't noticing or getting it! So, be thankful for my presence, and build a little algae or fungi pond in my honour – or treat yourself to some tasty mushrooms. They are all healthy ways to honour me! And do not step thoughtlessly into that fairy ring! It's all about me being in the right place... Don't ignore me! Right now, something really does need to be cleaned healthfully, before it begins to affect you."

The Angel de los Muertos speaks:

"I bring you a message from a loved one: one who has left already, but whose date of passing is drawing nearer. I ask you now to acknowledge your loved ones who are resting, in spirit, or creating new selves for their souls. You may soon be about to meet a beloved in a new form: I ask you to stay open-minded about the form in which the souls can come, and I ask you to be open to the message from the loved ancestors. For they have something to tell you, and it will come to you soon, in a vision, or a dream, or a message during a day dream that will bring such sweet tangible proof of what some people still call life after death. There is no death. There is only life, and a resting time, and change. Be ready to be comforted, and to learn more of the world beyond this world, which is always with you, but is not always believed in, or trusted, even when we send messages to you, as clear as a flag in the sky."

Strangely Lonely speaks:

"You are holding so tightly to something that it is proving to be a barrier between you and others – which is why you feel so alone at times. At present, you may need to open up just a little, and admit that you crave like-minded people around you – and this does not mean people who do the same things for a living as you – it means people who speak to your soul. You're craving metaphysical and mysterious discussions, and you've got some questions that truly need answers – or at least an exploration. It's time to consult Oracles – the ones that we find when we seek out friends who tell us what they see, not what they think we wish to hear. And what you are likely to hear is that you must let something go."

The Violet Duchess speaks:

"In your admirable quest for balance, you can actually become too neutral, pretending to be serene, acting polite, not making waves – and not speaking your truth!. Now I've arrived, showing you exactly how you feel, it's time to discover – or rediscover – a raw and honest emotional reaction you had to a person, or an issue, and express it. It's all very well being a lover of harmony, and not wanting to be a "troublemaker" but being a lukewarm person in regards to situations that really matter is not going to do you any favours. Bottling up your true self in turn leads to unhealthy relationships, aches, pains and even illness! When I show up, go for the passionate and truthful option – and rediscover just how strongly you can feel, and how much fun you can have!"

Amara speaks:

"Aloha! It is time for a guilt-free time-out for you, where you will invite the energy of Hawaii, and more self-nurturing into your life. It is time to discover and fade out those voices that say you must always work hard, and be stressed; to achieve what it is you wish for. I am of a time and a place where time moves in its own way, where you are at one with the natural world, and one where your body and soul are entwined, in unison, and singing the most beautiful song! You need the power of sunshine on your body: please give yourself a sunbath, a natural energetic healing of pure golden light, and feel the radiance warm your bones and fill you with joy!"

The Fairy of the Highlands speaks:

"I do not want to fight: I want to resolve disputes peacefully. But I will fight, if I must. And I am here to show you that you too must stand up for yourself, even though you almost chronically avoid conflict. Because of your tendency to avoid conflict, your peaceful nature is being taken advantage of. It is now time for you to take up this sword, to take a stand, speak the truth and not back down until a change has been made. To you, fighting for what you deserve may seem unnatural, wrong, or even frightening, and this little fairy knows it. But you are now being asked to protect what you have worked so hard to create. Take a stand. Hold up your sword. Do not back down. Then get ready to celebrate your victory!"

The Angel of Alchemy speaks:

"I am here to help you make a miraculous shift in your body and your health. Whether it is an injury or an illness, or simply feeling ill at ease within the form you currently have, I am the Angel of Alchemy and I can show you how to change your current experience of physicality. I stand here and have done so for many thousands of years. I have seen the fear and the guilt of others. I have seen the fear of infection, the anguish of pain, and the despair at life seeming to end. But I am here with you now to show you how to create health, and strength, and how to stop being so frightened of growing older and having times when your body will challenge you. All will be well, and all this will pass. This form is just one of many you will create. Let me show you how to live anew, with love and health."

Voodoo in Blue speaks:

"You are doing so well right now that you may begin to attract some attention from people who are, quite simply, opportunistic. And you are being "kind" and wish to help, and so I am going to step in and give you a very clear warning! I don't mind if I look like the "bad guy". What matters is that you get the message! Time to do a little stay-away magic, and while I won't be sending them bad thoughts – after all, there are no pins in my voodoo doll – you, if you take my advice, won't be asking them to come round for tea any time soon. Your feelings are right on this one. You know what to do. Don't get involved, and don't get bullied. You may have to snarl a little to get them to stay away too!"

The Violet Angel speaks:

"There have been times recently when you feel you've lost your spark, and that your physical body has just been exhausted – almost as if you were born tired! It has been a long night of the soul, but now I am here to let you know that not only has the "worst" past, the best is on the horizon. It is faint, and it is gathering energy, but it is on its way. Soon, with this new dawn, your energy will begin to flow again, and you'll feel reconnected to your own internal power source once more. Your spirit will blossom, and your intuition will hum! Please awaken earlier, and be ready to begin our work on this new project by spending time outside in nature in the early morning!"

The Lantern Fairy speaks:

"Sometimes, people say you should be cautious about where information is coming from. And that is indeed true. I am simply holding up the lantern I carry, and gently letting you see the likely outcome of the decisions you are making, and offering a clear solution to the problem at hand. Something has come to an end. A true end, and you have, as they say, hit the wall. You could try digging under it, or climbing over it, or you could try taking down the wall brick by brick. But if you follow me, I can show you a place where the wall has already come down, and where you can move through this obstacle without pain. Do not think this is cheating: there have been others who have come this way, and while you can tread the path the way you wish, I can help you make the breakthrough, find the passageway you are looking for. My guidance is safe, clear, and gentle. I am not here to send you in a false direction. I am here to clear the way, and light the path. It is up to you whether you make it harder than it needs to be. I'll show you the way. Trust me."

The Sewer Mermaid speaks:

"I am here to show you how to make sex and sensuality fun, playful, light-hearted and beautiful again, and to remove it from the great underneath you have placed it within. I will show you how to see your body as a place of delight and strength, and great spirit, and I will never die nor go away, no matter what you have been told, no matter what you have told yourself, and no matter what your society has told you. I am the wild free goddess self and you long for me to return to you. And so I am back, but I am showing you where you have put me all this time. Let's clean up our physical act. Let's love all aspects of the physical self. Let us not hide and repress anymore."

The Carousel Fairy speaks:

"Here I come again! It seems you need another cosmic reminder of something that needs to be cleared! Letting go is this moment's Very Important lesson for you to learn. I'm not suggesting forgetting – because where's the wisdom in that? But I am suggesting that you move on and actively replace this experience with completely different versions of the same theme. You must reconnect with the opportunities you have – staying attached to old patterns will simply make them come round again! Like this – wheee!"

The Strange Valentines speak:

"You have an enormous amount of cosmic help at the moment: and it's all focusing on the area of your love life. You will soon receive very good news regarding a relationship. You will also do a lot of work on healing old wounds from past relationships, especially past long term, serious relationships. Now, some of this news may not seem so great at the time. But please give yourself a chance to absorb the lessons, because you are moving into a beautiful new phase of your romantic life, where you will be free to create a wonderful new love life for yourself. Coming...very...soon!"

Death & The Maiden speaks:

"There is a very out of balance relationship in your life at present. You have been drawn into the drama, colour and entertainment of a relationship that is full of highs and lows and passion, but you are now discovering that is also draining, tiring and lacking in respect. It is time to truthfully assess this affair and take strong steps to be safer, more protected and more respected within it. If this cannot be done, remember that freedom is worth the pain of separation. Most of all, at this time you must ask yourself if this relationship is healthy for you. If the answer is no, then you must take firm steps to go."

Shallow Grave speaks:

"It is time to let something go, but before you do, let's take a moment to acknowledge what this was to you, know that this person meant so much, and that by returning them to the past, rather than yearning for them in the present, you are creating a future that has a greater freedom to it. There are opportunities for fresh starts all the time. Every day, in a sense, gives us a clean slate. For you, this sense of starting over is immensely important after you have grieved. You need to feel that something has been laid to rest, and will no longer trespass on the present. Life is kind of like that – so much of what happens isn't about what's actually happening – but thankfully, you will blossom and grow with fresh relationships and love after mourning this lost one."

Two Little Witches speak:

"Out, out and from within
We cleanse this space from trouble and din
Out, out, let all begone
And make this place a cheerful home!
We are here to cleanse and clean,
we are creatures in-between.
We will work from dusk till dawn,
to ensure energy is reborn.
We leave it clear, and bright, and blank
And for this task we ask no thanks.
But we do wish you well in this
May all brought in create your bliss!"

The Lady with a Bosch Egg speaks:

"My town is on fire, the night sky is full of screams and smoke, and I have done what I can to safeguard this treasure from the sacred library. I will keep it safe, record its wisdom, and ensure that these truths stay alive for a future time. I hope that you understand the history of the knowledge you crave, and respect and acknowledge the freedom of the times you now live in, and do the work yourself. It may be that at some time you too will find my egg, and that you are the person chosen to speak of the knowledge others thought was lost. Or it may be that you too are a guardian of wisdom: if you are, know when to keep silent, know what to keep to yourself, and know that some secrets come to light at the right time. I bring you now the symbols of the alchemists, the secrets of the Gnostics, and the wisdom of the magicians and the witches and the herbalists...all saved for this time, in this strange form of the egg."

Sea Storm being speaks:

"You are surrounded by storms, wild moments and a great deal of emotional drama at this time. The world you know may be changing in almost unrecognisable ways. There is destruction behind you, and you have left it in the past, but you are still searching for your new home. You will find it if you turn inwards and listen to the inner knowledge that will send you in the right direction. Don't "look"...look. I have shown up for you today to help you make it through this time with no land, no home and no apparent rescue. Trust in me."

She who wears the Dress of Alchemy speaks:

"It is time for you to celebrate who you truly are at this time, to acknowledge you have some energetic debris that needs to be cleared, and when you do this, the gold of who you truly are will shine through, just as these alchemical symbols shine from my dress. It is no longer possible in this new energy to hide who we are. We must take the time to be truly ourselves. There is no cloak to hide within, as you can see, this dress I wear reveals all my magicks and all my secrets. The secrets and the wisdoms of the ages are being revealed more now than ever before. When you have cleared your energy field of the guilt, the fear, the jealousy and the envy, you will be able to shine brightly too."

The Haunted Girl speaks:

"These faceless ones are coming to me, trying to take advantage of what they see as my moment of weakness – but I do not fear them, as I know they are blank, formless, and simply taking on any energy they can find. I know who I am, and I clearly see that they do not. They are simply spirits who have lost their way, and so they feed off others. I may not be at my strongest at this time, but I am stronger than they ever will be! They will not feed off me, for I know who they are, and what it is they seek. I do not wish them harm, but neither will I give my energy away to them. I will also warn you to do the same."

The Storm Angel speaks:

"There is nothing wrong, at all, with difference: diversity is wonderful. Shadows and light are beautiful and necessary and can co-exist in harmony. But certain kinds of difference do not blend...like oil and water, they separate and cannot co-exist in harmony. Therefore, I bring change, and when change comes for some it is simple, easy and flowing, for others, dramatic, erratic, wild and full of static! Like I said, I appear when two forms of energy collide: high and low! I then appear to burn away the old and create a clear, fresh vibration, where all that is stale, and fearful, and unpleasant has been cleared away! The wonderful thing about this challenging collision is that while you'll be nudged out of your comfort zone, you'll also realise just how much has changed, and how far you have come! The results will be worth the pressure – trust me!"

The Mend-a-Broken-Heart Fairy speaks:

"You have been hurt, and this heart feels bruised to me. It may have been what is called a lovers' quarrel, unrequited love, it may have been a break-up, and it may be that an adventure in love has turned harsh... but I am here to help you mend, and I will not let your broken heart bleed. I will wash (clear), heal (balance), and place the bandage over the wound (protection) and send you the healing that means deep, restful sleep and peace returns to you. I want you to take it easy on the path of love for now...soon you will feel your vitality return. But for now, it's a time of rest!"

The Candy Cane Angel speaks:

"You know what my problem is? And you know what your problem is? No? Well, let me tell you. OUR problem is that we both feel guilty about giving ourselves pleasure. See this little treat in my hands? It's not bad, is it? It's not evil, is it? But can I bring myself to just sit down and taste every moment of its sugary sweet delights? No. I have to wonder if it's the right time. If I have done enough to earn this treat. To wonder why I should get this when so many do not have a single candy cane for their own selves! I torment myself with these things – and so do you! How about we make a deal? Next time you ponder a gift to yourself: a massage, a treat, a spiritual workshop, a delicious meal, time to laugh with a friend, a long rest or nap, meditation time, a space clear...but with all of these necessities, you energetically tell yourself "I am way too busy for that indulgence", know you are really saying, "I do not deserve that!" Well, let's decide that we do! Now, I am about to have my treat. I now charge you with the same quest! Give yourself that which you have been denying yourself! You DO deserve it!"

The Carnivorous Greenhouse speaks:

"Am I not beautiful? Wouldn't you like to come a little closer? I am sure you will appreciate my beauty once you are able to see me properly. And no, of course I won't hurt you! I am just, after all, a plant... I may look like an innocent girl in a room full of green and living beings: and I am. But my nature is to devour, as is theirs. And so, before you decide to step into this room with me, and to work with this energy, know that you may be meeting a devouring one, one who consumes, who takes, who delights in watching the predatory actions of others, who dominates, controls, criticises and judges. I will eat what I can, and I will eat what comes near me. It is my nature. And although some may promise you they will not; if it is their nature to do such things, it is inevitable that they will do so! Do not forget who they are; and do not try to make them what they are not; or change and save them with your love. They will eat you. And delight in doing so."

The Clockwork Pumpkin speaks:

"I may look a strange muse, a clockwork pumpkin accompanied by a beautiful girl, but have no doubt: I am the new idea, the epiphany, the moment of clarity when the seeming chaos of life suddenly rearranges itself into a brilliant opportunity. You are about to be presented with such a golden idea that I want you to be ready. It may come from within you, or it may come from outside of you, but you have drawn it to you with the power of attraction and manifestation, and it is an idea that will bring you great riches of the body, mind and spirit. It is time to activate your own brilliant abilities and become the abundant, enriched being you were born to be! We are so pleased we have found you – we have waited for exactly the right being to take on this idea and bring it to life within the world! It has evolved out of time, out of space, and is perfect for you. It may be a song, a project, a new job, a relationship – its form is fluid, but its time is now, and you are the person chosen to bring it through! Cosmic duty it may be, but joy and love it will bring, as well as abundance and true happiness!"

The Angel of Time speaks:

"I'm getting straight to the point here, because someone really has to tell you. Stop giving so much to your work. All your time. Your energy. Your passion. Take better care of your health. This is the time to fulfil all those promises you've made to yourself, but barely even made the effort to keep. Meditate, eat well, take up gentle exercise and change unhealthy emotional patterns that are compromising your well-being – these are the challenges you need to set yourself. Gaze into a candle's flame, write down one true thing you love about all of your friends, and pay close attention to all the messages your body sends you – then make the changes you know it needs. I thank you in advance, for a happy you makes this world a far better place."

The Nautilus Princess speaks:

"I know I am strong, but, most people think of me as gentle, kind and good. Now I am to be the Ruler, what if they see me as power-hungry, dominating, greedy or controlling? Whatever the thoughts of those around me, there will be change as I change, and I will continue to hold fast to my nautilus, as it ever reminds me to grow in ways that are in tune with my purpose, my integrity, and what I feel is right. I vow to be steadfast and true, despite the challenges that are heading my way. I vow not to mis-use my power. But use it I will, and as a result I, like you, will grow in ways that are in tune with my true self, and true purpose."

The Girl surrounded by Ghosts of the Past speaks:

"Former friends, once upon a time lovers or even familiar situations may be about to visit you again! You have life themes and challenges and patterns too – the trick this time is to move through them swiftly, and leave them behind for good. These ghosts with their masks are here to show you what or who needs to be removed from your life – and they could include false beliefs you have about your own abilities, too. With this message, you now know it is Judgement Day, and you are powerful enough to put influences behind you, once and for all. Take off your mask and reveal all of who you are – for you have changed, and this change is worth showing to all who believe they know you."

The Pink Lotus Fairy speaks:

"On your journey, on your quest, there are times when it is worth finding that very heavenly place within where the soul of love resides. In this blissful state, this nirvana you'll be nurturing, some new, very enriching and exciting information and guidance will come to you. It would be very helpful for you to take up yoga, pilates or a physical exercise that has a spiritual practice attached to it in order to cultivate your inner peace, and to receive these messages clearly. Soon a teacher, guide or person who is a mentor will enter your life. When you meet them, know they are here to demonstrate ways for you to find your own path, and to grow and evolve into the being you are meant to be. Go within, look deeply into your heart, and find the love that overflows in its secret, quiet places. Your love is rich, and warm, and flowing still, and it is time for you to renew your connection to the source via the teachings you will be introduced to soon. When you patiently learn from a good teacher, who is pure in their intent, your powers of focus, telepathy, intuition and inner peace, no matter what the outer circumstances, will be greatly amplified."

The Fairy of the Green World speaks:

"The green world is changing, and I am asking for your help. The world needs you to tend the green things in it in some way right now – and it is your time to make a contribution. Time to plant a garden, assist another with theirs, or share some food, flowers or herbs from your own. Develop your connection to solar energy, find your own water source, and depend less on supermarkets, ATMs and electricity. Learn to live with her, the soul of the green world. By providing the world with this beautiful example you are nourishing and nurturing our mother the Earth, who feels so tired some days! Find a forest, or a grove of trees, or a fairy ring of mushrooms, somewhere that speaks to your soul and sit with her a while. When she breathes her messages through the leaves and whispers the words of wisdom into your ears, you will know the right place and time to devote this sacred donation of time and energy. I thank you in advance. The fairies will be sure to help you in return!"

The Witch at the End of the World speaks:

"I am not wicked, but I am a witch, and changes are made when the world bends and shifts. I hold this hourglass up to you now so you know that the time for an ending is almost upon us. You can see the signs all about you – the strange weather, the hurricanes, the cyclones, the earth changes all about us – but so many simply say I am wicked for showing you this. They blame me for what they call the catastrophes, and they ignore the signs. They are with you, and it is time to be ready. We are all about to experience a huge change – and it will be for the better. But while we hold onto the old, the storms will blast us, and the land will shift, and self-healing will look like destruction."

About the Author

Lucy Cavendish works magick every single day of her life, embracing it as a creed for personal fulfillment and happiness, and as a belief system that sees us as part of nature, and thus gives us all the motivation to respect and revere and delight in our unique experience here on Planet Earth.

Some of Lucy's other bestselling publications include *Oracle of the Dragonfae*, *Les Vampires*, *Oracle of the Shapeshifters*, *Oracle of the Mermaids*, *Wild Wisdom of the Faery Oracle* and *The Lost Lands*.

Apart from regular television and radio appearances, she is a feature writer for 'Spellcraft Magazine', 'Spheres', and has appeared in anthologies like 'Disinformation's Pop Goes The Witch!' In 1992, Lucy created Witchcraft magazine, which she edited for five years.

She is a classic book witch and adores writing, reading and creating enchanted workshop experiences. Lucy Cavendish currently lives in Sydney with her pixie-like daughter and the spirit of her beautiful labradoodle dog.

Visit Lucy's website at: **www.lucycavendish.com**

About the Artist

Jasmine Becket-Griffith is a world-renowned fantasy artist. Born in 1979, she has spent all of her adult life working as a fine artist, painting traditionally by hand with acrylic paints. Her artwork can be found in private collections and public displays throughout the world. Jasmine's paintings blend realism with wide-eyed wonder – exploring gothic themes, with elements of classical literature, the occult, nature and fantasy – and of course, faeries!

Jasmine's paintings appear in countless books (notably *The World of Faery* with Alan Lee, *The Art of Faery* with Brian Froud, *Spectrum 11*, *Spectrum 13*, *Gothic Art Now*, *Big Eye Art: Resurrected and Transformed* and her four solo art books *Strangeling: The Art of Jasmine Becket-Griffith*, *Fairy*, *Jasmine Becket-Griffith: Porfolio Volume I* and *Portfolio Volume II*). Her work also graces many television shows and movies, magazines and advertisements, tattoo parlours, themeparks, and of course her range of hundreds of different licensed merchandise products (distributed chain stores such as Hot Topic, Torrid, and Target/Super Target) as well as lines of collectibles through the Bradford Exchange and Hamilton Collection. Jasmine's official website and online gallery can be seen at www.strangeling.com and she also has an eBay store under the seller ID 'strangeling'.

Jasmine lives in beautiful Celebration, Florida with her husband/assistant Matt and their cats.

For more information on this
or any Blue Angel Publishing release,
please visit our website at:

www.blueangelonline.com